THE MERCHANT OF VENICE

by
William Shakespeare

Teacher Guide

Written by
Gloria Levine, M. A.

Note

The text used to prepare this guide was the Signet Classic edition published by the Penguin Group, Sylvan Barnet, General Editor. If other editions are used, scene and line numbers may vary.

Please note: Please assess the appropriateness of this play for the age level and maturity of your students prior to reading and discussing it with your class.

ISBN 1-58130-566-4

To order, contact your local school supply store, or—

Novel Units, Inc.
P.O. Box 791610
San Antonio, TX 78279

Web site: www.educyberstor.com

Table of Contents

Plot Summary

Bassanio falls in love with the lovely, wealthy Portia and asks his friend Antonio for a loan so that he can marry her. Antonio's wealth is tied up in his ships, which are at sea, so he agrees to sign a note for his friend. Shylock, a Jewish moneylender, gives Bassanio 3,000 ducats with the understanding that Antonio will give a pound of flesh if he fails to repay the loan in three months. When the ships sink, Shylock demands his pound of flesh, but Portia disguises herself as a lawyer and saves the day (for Antonio). Shylock, on the other hand, loses all—including his daughter and his faith.

Background on the Playwright

Shakespeare's exact birthdate is unknown, but he was baptized on April 26, 1564, in Stratford-on-Avon, England. His father, John, was a prosperous wool, leather, and grain merchant, as well as a town official. His mother, Mary, was the daughter of a gentleman farmer. It is known that young William attended school and studied Latin and literature. In 1582, he married Anne Hathaway, a woman eight years his senior. They had three children: a daughter, Susanna, and twins, Hamnet and Judeth.

In 1586, Shakespeare left Stratford to become the stage manager of "The Theatre" in London, so named because it was the only theatre in town. He soon joined the acting company of The Theatre, and with Richard Burbage and William Kemp he performed at court in many plays.

Shakespeare's earliest works were produced in 1591-02, including several of the histories and *Love's Labour's Lost, Two Gentlemen of Verona,* and *Comedy of Errors.* In 1592, he wrote *Romeo and Juliet.* It was followed in quick succession by *The Merchant of Venice, A Midsummer Night's Dream, All's Well That Ends Well, The Taming of the Shrew,* and *The Merry Wives of Windsor.*

Shakespeare made an important business move in 1599 when he joined Richard Burbage and several other actors to build the Globe Theatre. He was a shareholder in the Globe and a part-owner of a company of actors called Lord Chamberlain's Company, later known as The King's Men.

Many of Shakespeare's plays were produced at the Globe, where he had both financial security and a first-rate acting company to produce his plays. This was his greatest writing period. In 1599-1600, he wrote *Much Ado About Nothing, As You Like It,* and *Twelfth Night.* Between 1600 and 1611, he wrote the tragedies for which he is so well remembered: *Julius Caesar, Hamlet, Othello, Macbeth, King Lear,* and *Antony and Cleopatra,* among others. During this time he also wrote 154 sonnets which were published in 1609. Late in 1608 or 1609, Shakespeare and his partners purchased the Blackfriars Theatre to use as a winter location for play production.

In 1611, at the height of his fame and popularity, Shakespeare moved back to Stratford. His son died at this time. He sold out his interests in London, although he did continue to write and travel to the city until his death in 1616. Not until 1623 was an edition of his collected plays published in what is now called the First Folio.

The Globe Theatre

Obtain a picture of the Globe Theatre to show your class, or use an educational kit to build a small model so students can see the various areas of the theatre as they are discussed in class.

Physical Aspects

The Globe had three levels set on a large platform, open to the sky. The stage jutted out into the audience on three sides. The building itself was octagon-shaped (eight-sided). A cross-section of the London population typically attended. For one cent, a theatre-goer could stand or sit on the ground (hence, the name "groundling"). Two cents would buy a seat in the galleries and elsewhere. The noblemen paid nothing, and were seated in the lord's rooms near the stage. Plays were always performed during the day, as there were no lights. A flag was flown on top of the theatre on days when a play was to be given.

Setting/Staging

Plays were performed at the Globe Theatre with little or no interruption. There were no curtains to signal the end of an act, although there was a "tiring house," a room where actors could change costumes or stay out of view when they were not on stage. The settings were given through action and dialogue. The actors soliloquies and asides made the audience feel particularly involved, as the actors seemed to be talking directly to the audience. Actors' entrances and exits were seen openly by the audience through two doors on either side of the stage.

The Actors

Senior actors got the major parts in plays. They were experienced and often held shares in the theatre company. Hired men, who were paid weekly and held no shares, held backstage jobs and played minor parts in the plays. Boy actors played the roles of women and children.

Note: We used the Signet Classic edition of *The Merchant of Venice* to prepare this guide. References are made by act, scene, and line number. If you use a different edition, particularly one that has been abridged or rephrased, these references may vary.

Initiating Activities

Choose one or more of the following activities to prepare students for the play they are about to study.

1. Prereading Discussion

Of Commitment: What is a commitment? What are some examples of commitments? What commitments have you made? Which do you think are the most important ones? When is it okay to break a commitment? When is it okay to break your word?

Of Marriage: What should two people know about each other before marriage? How much say should parents have in who their child marries? What do you think are the "ingredients" for a happy marriage? How has the woman's role in a marriage changed since Shakespeare's time? In what ways is it the same? What "tests" do you think the person you marry will have to pass? Do you think a person owes more loyalty to his/her marital partner than to his/her other close friends?

Of Loss: What are some of the losses most of us experience? How do people cope with loss? What are some reasons for loss of religious faith? loss of hope? loss of money? loss of happiness?

Of Mercy and Justice: What is mercy? Who deserves mercy? What are some merciful acts you know of? When have you shown mercy to someone else? Have you ever "put yourself on someone's mercy"? What is justice? Can there be justice without mercy? Can there be mercy without justice? Does our court system allow for both? Do you personally value one over the other?

Of Shakespeare: What do you know about Shakespeare? When did he live? Why did he become so famous? Which of his plays and poems are you familiar with? What were some of the women in his stories like?

2. Anticipation Guide

Have students rate and discuss statements that apply to themes and events in the play. For example:

You should never break your word.
Anti-Semitism has been around for thousands of years.
Men don't like assertive women.
A good friend is someone who would die for you.
Forgive and forget.
An eye for an eye.
Friends and lovers don't mix.
We are all products of our environment.

3. Debate

Have students who agree with the following statement get on one side of the room; those who disagree get on the other; undecided students remain in the middle as the other students try to "win them over."

"Revenge is sweet."

4. Background Information

It is important to understand the cultural subtext for the anti-Semitism woven throughout the play. Many critics feel that Shakespeare's Shylock is a caricature of the Jew—and a reflection of the rabid anti-Semitism of the time, from which Shakespeare was not immune. A minority of critics do maintain that Shakespeare was 400 years ahead of his time—engaged in an anti-Semitic crusade. These critics point out that 50 years after the play was published, Jews were invited back into England, ending over 300 years of banishment. Perhaps, say these critics, *The Merchant of Venice* was to anti-Semitism what *Uncle Tom's Cabin* was to slavery. In any case, it was **illegal** in Shakespeare's day to be a Jew—as it had been throughout much of Europe during the Middle Ages. The only occupation a Jew was legally entitled to pursue in Shakespeare's time was that of moneylender. Most Elizabethans had little first-hand knowledge of Jews (Jews had been expelled from England in 1290), but small segregated groups remained in Shakespeare's England, and Jews were certainly not unknown. Indeed, Shakespeare would have been well-aware of the execution of Dr. Roderigo Lopez—a converted Portuguese Jew accused of plotting to poison the Queen. The Elizabethans' image of Jews was generally steeped in misconception. For instance, it was commonly held that Jewish men menstruated and that as part of their religious ritual, Jews crucified Christian children and drank their blood. The conversion of Jewish girls (seen in this play when Shylock's daughter marries a Christian) was a common, early-modern European (Christian) fantasy.

5. Book Talk/Summary

Many educators feel that the goal of studying Shakespeare is to bring the play alive—and that students as directors/actors should learn to make decisions about how the play is presented—*not* spend a lot of time figuring out what the play means. Peggy O'Brien of the Folger Shakespeare Library in Washington, DC suggests that the teacher simply tell the story—with key lines from the play interspersed. [For this storytelling, teachers might read aloud the version by Charles and Mary Lamb (Tales from Shakespeare) or the summaries included in this guide.] Pairs of students might be given lines to speak on cue—with movement or gesture—as the story is told. (The Lamb version is ideal for this, as it contains many of Shakespeare's lines.)

6. Audio/Video

To sensitize students to Shakespeare's language before they begin their own oral reading, have them listen to or view a selected scene from it—such as Portia's "quality of mercy" speech—4.1.183-204). Have students speculate about the scene. What is Portia saying? Do you agree with her? What is her tone? How does she seem to feel about the merchant whom she is addressing? How is the language in this scene different from the language we use today?

7. Acting

Hand out copies of a speech from the play (such as Portia's speech, see #6 above). Have several students do a choral reading (stand up and read it aloud together). Ask: What does the speech seem to tell you about Portia? about "the Jew" (Shylock)?

Have students work in collaborative groups to act and direct particular scenes throughout the play. Remember: If students are to develop a love of Shakespeare, you have to get them up on their feet! Shakespeare never intended his plays to be published and studied as literature!

8. Response Log

Have students keep a response log as they read and perform the play. Students should jot down brief summaries and reactions to each section of the play after they read. These reactions might begin: "I don't understand...," "Portia reminds me of...," "I don't think Shylock should...," etc.

9. Geography

Have students find the setting (Venice) on a map. Have students locate other places (Morocco, Aragon) as they are mentioned in the story.

10. Prediction

Before viewing and/or reading the play, present students with a list of statements describing one of the characters in the play. Then have students verbally "flesh out" the description (by providing other phrases that probably apply to the character) and pencil-sketch the character (or find a magazine cut-out) as they imagine him or her for later comparison with Shakespeare's creation.

Sample list for Portia:

- daughter of a rich, deceased gentleman
- assertive
- responsible
- devoted to her father
- outspoken
- talented
- virtuous
- acute
- desirable

What other qualities does Portia probably have? What sort of person do you think Portia will fall in love with?

11. Role Play

Before handing out copies of the play, have students break into small groups to discuss or do improvisations of the following situations, analagous to events in the story.

(a) You're on a TV game show, trying to choose among three "doors" to find the one that hides the winning gift: a gold one that says "gain here what many desire," a silver one that promises "as much as you deserve behind this door," and a lead one that warns, "you must risk all you have for what's here." Reason out loud as you make your choice.

(b) You are the judge in an unusual case. A researcher wants to be awarded "custody" of the ape she has taught sign language, but the law is behind the institution where she works—which wants to send the ape to a medical research facility. Your sympathies lie with the ape and the researcher with whom she has bonded, so you try to convince the head of the institution to show some mercy.

(c) A girl wants to go shopping at the mall with her boyfriend but she has no money—and her father, who has forbidden her to see the boyfriend, isn't about to give her any money, if she asks. The girl and her boyfriend plan how to get around her father.

Students in the "audience" should take notes on the role-play/discussion and compare their notes later with what happens in *The Merchant of Venice*.

12. Introduction

To introduce any play by Shakespeare, Hester Zimmerman (*English Journal*, November 1988) suggests choosing a pivotal scene from the play, (such as 3.2.1-39, where Portia introduces Bassanio to the coffer test).

a) Delete character names, stage directions, punctuations, unnecessary lines.
b) Distribute the result to students. Have students read the scene out loud, taking turns with different speeches.
c) Repeat the reading.
d) Ask students questions of varying difficulty about the scene—beginning with "What is the relationship between these characters? What problem do they face?") (For other ideas, see the discussion questions in this guide.)
e) Have students discuss and punctuate several speeches in groups (after explaining that any editions we have today were punctuated by editors).
f) Have students add stage directions that mention gestures, props.
g) Students decide as a group which of several hats best fits each character's personality.
h) Have students block the scene (decide where actors will move, how they will speak their lines).
i) Have each of the three or four groups enact the scene, and then discuss differences in performance.
j) Finally watch a video or actual performance of the play to find out one director's interpretation of what "really happened." Remind students that interpretations—and even punctuation of the scenes—vary.

13. Labeling

Instruct students to watch for places in the play where characters change or mask their true identity and mark these with an I. Alternatively, have students mark places where characters make (M) or break (B) commitments. These passages are then available to students as supportive evidence during discussion and writing about the play.

14. Verbal Scales

After students finish various scenes in the play, have them chart their judgments of Shylock, Antonio, and Portia using the following scales—or others you construct. Students should discuss their ratings with evidence from the play.

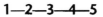

dominating	submitting
being him/herself	pretending
merciful	merciless
concerned for others	self-centered
witty	humorless
spirited	broken

Vocabulary Activities

See the **Novel Units Student Packet** for *The Merchant of Venice* for several reproducible vocabulary activities.

Vocabulary words are grouped in this guide by scene, with Act.scene.line numbers given after each word. As you assign various portions of the play, have students practice reading aloud at home before each class. Discuss particular vocabulary words only after students have encountered the words in their Shakespearean context. Focus on two types of words: those that we rarely hear today and those that are common today—but whose meanings have changed. In addition to the entries at the bottom of each page in the text, you might use one of the several Shakespearean dictionaries on the Internet.

1. The following is one tried-and-true method of approaching the vocabulary in Shakespeare's plays.
   - Select a short passage.

   - Next, have students paraphrase the passage (placing the passage in context by explaining what is happening in relation to what came before).

   - Finally, have students define target words in the passage (difficult, either because they are archaic or have a meaning different from the one with which students are familiar).

2. Explain that Shakespeare used (and made up) many words that are now rare or obsolete—some quite strange-sounding to the modern ear! Present students with a list of such words from *The Merchant of Venice* and have them guess what the meanings might be.

Sample list:

moe (1.1.108)	gudgeon (1.1.102)	dumbshow (1.2.72)	eanlings (1.3.76)
doit (1.3.137)	martlet (2.9.27)	forespurrer (2.9.94)	knapped (3.1.9)
shrowd (3.2.243)	bankrout (4.1.122)		

3. Instruct students to find words in the play that look familiar—but mean something different today. Have them a) read the word in its Shakespearean context, and b) explain what it means—and how that differs from today's meaning.

For example:

patch (2.5.45)	close (2.6.47)	discover (2.7.1)	estimation (2.7.26)
disabling (2.7.30)	gentle (2.7.78)	villain (2.8.4)	reasoned (2.8.27)
straight (2.9.1)	fond (2.9.26)	schedule (2.9.54)	likely (2.9.91)
envious (3.2.282)	remorse (4.1.20)	strange (5.1.278)	

4. Have students group words from the Shakespearean vocabulary list below into two categories—those that look familiar (although today's meaning may be different) and those that are no longer commonly used. Then have them fill out a chart like the one that follows the list.

methoughts (1.3.66)   rheum (1.3.114)   nay (2.2.75)   knave (2.3.12)
wherefore (2.5.12)   patch (2.5.45)   gentle (2.7.78)   cozen (2.9.37)
smug (3.1.43)   cur (3.3.18)   accoutred (3.4.63)   remorse (4.1.20)
rehearsed (4.1.361)   unthrift (5.1.16)   paltry (5.1.147)   scrubbed (5.1.162)
strange (5.1.278)   bedfellow (5.1.284)

a. words that look familiar	today's meaning	Shakespeare's meaning

b. words that look "Shakespearean"	what I predict the meaning might be	what I discovered to be the actual meaning in the play

5. Have students bring in pictures or examples of some of the concrete terms, such as

argosies (1.1.9)   shaft (1.1.140)   death's-head (1.2.50) throstle (1.2.59)
ducats (1.3.62)   livery (2.1.2)   penthouse (2.6.1)   sepulcher (3.2.96)
rasher (3.5.24)   gaping pig (4.1.47)   patens (5.1.59)   Argus (5.1.230)

11

Act-by-Act

Act I

Scene I: Antonio is depressed. His friend Bassanio tells him that he is in love with a beautiful, rich woman named Portia and wants to get rid of his debts. Antonio replies that all of his fortunes are with his ships at sea, but he is willing to put up credit for his friend.

Scene II: Portia tells her maid, Nerissa, that she is feeling down. She is not happy about the three-chest "test" that her late father devised for her suitors. The one who chooses the right chest (of the gold, silver, and lead) with the right saying, wins Portia. Portia is not interested in any of the suitors. Nerissa says that Bassanio, on the other hand, is worthy of her lady, and Portia happily agrees.

Scene III: Bassanio, meanwhile, approaches Shylock, the Jewish usurer, about a loan. Shylock agrees to lend 3,000 ducats to Bassanio for three months, with Antonio bound. Shylock hates Antonio, who has in the past lent money for free—in contrast with Shylock's high interest rates—and who has spat at Shylock and spurned the Jewish people. Seemingly as a joke, Shylock adds a stipulation to the agreement: if he is not repaid on the given day, he will get a pound of Antonio's flesh; Antonio agrees, over Bassanio's protestations.

Vocabulary

sad (1.1.1)	want-wit (1.1.6)	argosies (1.1.9)	portly (1.1.9)
pageants (1.1.11)	cursy (1.1.13)	venture (1.1.15)	still (1.1.17)
roads (1.1.19)	ague (1.1.23)	gentle (1.1.32)	bechanced (1.1.38)
strange (1.1.51)	prevented (1.1.61)	jaundice (1.1.85)	entertain (1.1.90)
opinion (1.1.91)	gudgeon (1.1.102)	moe (1.1.108)	gear (1.1.110)
vendible (1.1.112)	something (1.1.124)	abridged (1.1.126)	rate (1.1.127)
gaged (1.1.130)	occasions (1.1.139)	shaft (1.1.140)	proof (1.1.144)
virtues (1.1.163)	seat (1.1.171)	thrift (1.1.175)	commodity (1.1.178)
troth (1.2.1)	surfeit (1.2.5)	sentences (1.2.10)	throstle (1.2.59)
doublet (1.2.73)	hose (1.2.74)	imposition (1.2.103)	sirrah (1.2.130)
publican (1.3.38)	gross (1.3.52)	methoughts (1.3.66)	eaning (1.3.84)
gaberdine (1.3.109)	rheum (1.3.114)	doit (1.3.137)	fearful (1.3.172)

(**Note:** It is recommended that you do a first-read-through of each scene in class with frequent pauses to figure out meanings. Encourage students to check the numbered notes at the bottom of each page. The discussion questions below will help clarify what is happening in the plot. Then do another run-through, complete with sound effects and simple props. Use diagrams included with the questions on the board.)

Discussion Questions

1. What "love story" has been introduced in Act I? *(Bassanio is in love with Portia.)* What fairy-tale-like elements have you noticed in the story so far? *(Portia's future husband must pass a test.)* What "test" has been devised for Portia's suitors? *(They must choose between three coffers—gold, silver, and lead.)* Why do you suppose Portia's late father devised this test? What do you suppose Portia thinks of the test?

2. What are your impressions of Shylock at this point? *(He seems angry, vengeful.)* What do his speech patterns show about him? *(His speech is abrupt, punctuated with earthy examples such as the story of Laban and the lambs.)* Why do Antonio and Shylock dislike each other so much? *(Antonio disapproves of the high interest Shylock charges for his loans.)* How, then, have they ended up making a business agreement? From Antonio's point of view, what are the pros and cons of borrowing from Shylock?

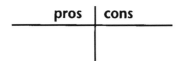

pros	cons

(Although Antonio dislikes borrowing from someone whose practices he considers unethical, Antonio has promised his friend Bassanio money he can't provide, himself.) What do you think of that agreement? In what tone do you imagine Shylock saying, "and, in a merry sport, If you repay me not on such a day...Be nominated for an equal pound..." (1.3.142-146)? Was he kidding, at that point?

3. What is Antonio like? *(restrained, generous, depressed)*

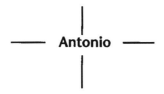

Antonio

Why is he depressed in the beginning? *(He seems to have a vague premonition.)* Do you think Solario, Solanio, Gratiano, or Bassanio understand him? What different approaches do they take to cheer him up? *(Solanio teases him about being in love; Salerio says he understands why Antonio would worry about his ships; Gratiano clowns around, tells Antonio not to act sad in order to seem wise.)* What would you say to him if he were your friend?

13

4. In this act, we begin to form our impressions of Bassanio—from his own words and actions and also from what others say about him. What picture of him is forming in your mind—and what clues contribute to that picture? Why do you suppose Antonio is so ready to help out Bassanio—apparently repeatedly? Why do you think Portia is attracted to him—and Nerissa believes he is a worthy suitor for her mistress?

5. What do you think of Portia? Does she remind you of any other characters you have met in Shakespeare's plays—or other literature? What sort of relationship does she have with Nerissa? *(Portia seems close to her maid.)* What does she seem to want in a husband?

6. What does this act reveal about Elizabethan attitudes toward Jews—or would you say that Shylock's Jewishness has little to do with his portrayal? Do you think Shakespeare is promoting a certain stereotype of Jews? *(Shylock as stingy-moneylender)*

7. What do you notice about the structure of this act? For instance, what similar threads run through the first two scenes? *(Bassanio tells his friend of his love for Portia, then Portia confides in her maid her interest in Bassanio.)* How are Antonio's and Portia's moods similar? *(Both feel somewhat bleak.)* Although these two haven't met each other, what links them? *(Nerissa)*

8. What do you notice about the way the act ends? *(Antonio and Bassanio speak in rhymes about the deal with Shylock.)* What is the impact of the rhyming couplets? What is the tone?

9. What is one of your favorite lines from this act? What is memorable about it? Do you think it contains one of the key ideas in the story? Is there something special about the way Shakespeare uses language here? Is it particularly witty? A very "quotable quote"?

Prediction
Will Antonio forfeit on the debt?

Supplementary Activities

Literary Analysis: Anti-hero
Shylock is considered by many critics to be an **anti-hero** rather than—villain (cruelly malicious person representing an evil agency in the plot). An anti-hero simply lacks the attributes that make him a heroic figure—such as nobility of mind and spirit.

Have students discuss why Shylock dislikes Antonio. Does he have solid reasons—or is this an example of inexplicable antipathy? What is behind his stipulation about the pound of flesh? Suggest that students revisit this question each time they meet Shylock in the play: Is Shylock truly evil?

Foreshadowing
Foreshadowing is a hint or suggestion of something that will happen later in a story. Explain that many of the Elizabethans believed in presentiments. Ask what sort of presentiment Antonio seems to have in this scene. (He is sad, for no apparent reason, and seems to expect something bad to happen.) Ask students how this heightens suspense. (We wonder whether something will happen to justify his melancholy.) Tell students to find out whether Antonio's presentiment is justified, as they read on.

Quotable Quotes
Point out that many quotes from this and other Shakespearean plays have entered into our everyday language. Ask what they think is the most "quotable quote" from this section—and why.

Writing Ideas
1. Write the conversation Portia may have had with her late father about the "test." He should explain why he feels the suitor test is necessary—and perhaps describe some alternative tests he has considered. Portia should explain why she feels the test is a good idea—or defend her ability to choose a suitable husband on her own.

2. Write Bassanio a letter of advice about the loan agreement he has made. Describe your own experience with loans—as a borrower or lender.

Act II

Scene I: At Belmont, Portia's residence, the Prince of Morocco arrives to take the test.

Scene II: Launcelot the (Jewish) Clown decides to run away from his master, Shylock. His blind old father, Gobbo, fails to recognize him. Bassanio hires Launcelot. Bassanio's friend, Gratiano, asks to come along with him to Belmont and promises to tone down his joking.

Scene III: Jessica tells Launcelot she will miss him and gives him a letter for Lorenzo. Jessica plans to become a Christian and marry Lorenzo.

Scene IV: Lorenzo pays Launcelot for bringing the letter in which Jessica tells him to come to her father's house to get her—and her father's gold and jewels. Salerio and Solanio go to prepare for the evening's masque.

Scene V: While calling for Jessica, Shylock warns Launcelot he will not be as happy with Bassanio as a boss. Shylock tells Jessica he is on his way to a dinner at Bassanio's so that he can satisfy his hatred. He instructs her to lock up the house if the masquers appear in the street below. Launcelot, however, takes her aside and tells her that Lorenzo will be among the masquers.

Scene VI: The masquers appear at Shylock's house and Jessica steps out, dressed as a boy. Antonio appears and Gratiano tells him he will be happy to sail to Belmont tonight.

Scene VII: At Portia's house, the Prince of Morocco shows up and chooses the gold casket, reasoning aloud with humility that while he may not deserve the lady (silver), all the world certainly desires her (gold). When he finds a death's head inside, he knows he has lost.

Scene VIII: Salerio and Solanio talk about how Shylock discovered his daughter's absence and went to search Bassanio's ship—too late, for it had sailed. Shylock has been going through the streets rambling about the loss of his daughter and his wealth. Salerio hopes that the shipwreck he heard about has nothing to do with Antonio's ships.

Scene IX: The pompous Prince of Aragon tries his hand at the caskets, wrongly choosing the silver since he assumes he deserves Portia.

Vocabulary

livery (2.1.2)	nice (2.1.14)	scanted (2.1.17)	marry (2.2.43)
halter (2.2.106)	anon (2.2.117)	gramercy (2.2.120)	cater-cousins (2.2.130)
proverb (2.2.148)	guarded (2.2.154)	scapes (2.2.164)	gear (2.2.165)
liberal (2.2.182)	habit (2.2.187)	civility (2.2.192)	ostent (2.2.193)
quaintly (2.4.6)	bid (2.5.7)	patch (2.5.45)	penthouse (2.6.1)
measures (2.6.11)	garnish (2.6.45)	close (2.6.47)	beshrow (2.6.52)
discover (2.7.1)	estimation (2.7.26)	disabling (2.7.30)	cerecloth (2.7.51)
complexion (2.7.79)	villain (2.8.4)	reasoned (2.8.27)	fraught (2.8.30)
slubber (2.8.39)	straight (2.9.1)	election (2.9.3)	fond (2.9.26)
martlet (2.9.27)	cozen (2.9.37)	gleaned (2.9.45)	schedule (2.9.54)
iwis (2.9.67)	wroath (2.9.77)	wit (2.9.80)	regreets (2.9.88)
likely (2.9.91)	forespurrer (2.9.94)	post (2.9.99)	

© Novel Units, Inc.

16

Discussion Questions

1. Why isn't Portia interested in most of the suitors? For instance, what do her comments about the Prince of Morocco show about her reasons for rejecting him? *(She is displeased by his skin color, for one thing.)* Would you say she is prejudiced—or just expressing preference for one type of man over another?

2. What is Launcelot's dilemma? *(His conscience tells him not to leave his master—"a kind of devil"—but if he follows his impulse to leave, he will be ruled by "the devil himself.")* Why do you think he wants to leave Shylock?

3. Why doesn't Launcelot's father recognize him? *(He is old and blind.)* What expression is turned on its head when Launcelot says, "It is a wise father that knows his own child"? *(It is a wise child that knows his own father.)* Why do you suppose Gobbo has been left out of several film adaptations of the play?

4. Gratiano wants to go to Belmont. Why? *(He is in love with Portia's maid, Nerissa.)* How does Bassanio ask him to change his behavior for the trip? *(Bassanio asks Gratiano to act more decorous.)* Have you ever asked a friend to tone down his or her behavior? Do you find it interesting that one of Bassanio's friends *(Antonio)* seems to have lost his capacity for mirth and another *(Gratiano)* seems to have that capacity in overabundance? Which character is the more sympathetic one?

5. Why does Jessica sneak away from her father? *(He would not approve of her marriage to a Christian.)* What would happen if she were to tell him of her plans to leave? Does she seem to have any regrets? Does she feel badly, at all, about leaving the man who has apparently raised her since her mother's death? Does she feel guilty, at all, about stealing from him? *(There is little evidence that she feels anything but excited.)* What is her disguise? *(She is disguised as a man.)*

6. Shylock refused Bassanio's dinner invitation in the previous act. Why do you think he has apparently changed his mind? *(vengefulness)* What does his dream seem to foreshadow? *(His dream of moneybags is a premonition of the loss of his daughter—and money.)*

7. What does Shylock mean when he says, "Fast bind, fast find, A proverb never stale in thrifty mind" (2.5.53-54)? *(Lock up what you have.)* How do these words confirm a common stereotype? What does Jessica mean when she says, after he is gone, "Farewell; and if my fortune be not crost, I have a father, you a daughter, lost" (lines 55-56)? *(She will marry Lorenzo, be cut off from her father.)* In what tone do you think she speaks these lines?

8. How do the Prince of Morocco's and the Prince of Aragon's approaches to the riddle differ? *(The Prince of Morocco is rather self-effacing—hoping that he deserves Portia, but going with gold—his admission that he desires her; Aragon is arrogant—choosing silver, on the assumption that he deserves her.)* Do you think Portia was any more sympathetic to one than the other? What would she have done if one or the other had chosen the right coffer?

9. Did you find anything puzzling about this act? To understand this act, what do you think is the single most important question to consider?

Prediction
Which casket will Bassanio choose—and why?

Supplementary Activities

Literary Analysis: Masque
The masque was a form of entertainment in England in the 16th and 17th centuries originally consisting of pantomime and dancing, but later including dialogue and song, presented in elaborate productions given by amateur and professional actors. Have students point out the references to a masque in this scene. *(Solario and Solanio prepare for a masque later that evening; Shylock instructs Jessica to close up the house if masquers appear in the streets.)*

Soliloquy
Soliloquy is the act of talking while or as if alone. A soliloquy consists of lines spoken by a character that are meant to represent the character's unspoken thoughts and feelings. While soliloquizing, the character ignores or is oblivious to any hearers present.

Point out the lines spoken by Jessica, alone on the stage, at the end of Act 2, Scene 5. What do these lines show about how Jessica is feeling? *(She is looking forward to the break from her father as she goes to Lorenzo.)*

Writing Ideas
1. You are Jessica. Write a letter to your best friend about how you have run off with Lorenzo. Describe your plan and explain why you put it into effect. Also, tell how you feel about both men—and about what you have done.

2. Write a soliloquy for Portia in which she muses aloud about two of her suitors—the Princes of Morocco and Aragon. Imagine that she is thinking about the conversation she might have had with her father—had he been alive.

Act III

Scene I: Salerio tells Solanio that Antonio's ships are lost. Shylock accuses Salerio of knowing about Jessica's flight and vows to feed his revenge by making Antonio honor his bond. (Here he gives his famous "Hath not a Jew eyes" speech.) Tubal reports to Shylock that, although he hasn't found Jessica, he has heard that Antonio's ships are wrecked. Jessica has been spending her father's gold and even traded her mother's ring—precious to Shylock—for a monkey. Shylock tells Tubal to meet him at the synogogue.

Scene II: At Belmont, Bassanio chooses the correct (lead) coffer and wins Portia, much to her delight. She gives him her ring, and he promises her that it will never leave his finger while he lives. Gratiano and Nerissa announce their engagement. Salerio arrives (with Lorenzo and Jessica) and gives Bassanio a letter from Venice with the shocking news that Antonio's ships have been lost. Jessica warns that her father has sworn to have Antonio's flesh. When Portia learns what Antonio owes Shylock, she offers to pay twice or three times that to settle the debt. She suggests that they get married right away so that Bassanio can return to be with Antonio in Venice.

Scene III: Shylock demands that Antonio honor the bond. Antonio gives up trying to protest and prepares to die.

Scene IV: Portia tells Lorenzo to look after the house while she is away (supposedly praying and meditating with Nerissa). Then she secretly sends her servant Balthasar to take a letter to her cousin, Doctor Bellario, in Padua and to pick up some papers and clothes from him.

Scene V: Jessica tells Launcelot she will be saved by her husband, who has made her a Christian. Launcelot criticizes Lorenzo, who accuses him of getting a Moorish woman pregnant. Lorenzo and Jessica go to dinner.

Vocabulary

gossip (3.1.6)	knapped (3.1.9)	betimes (3.1.19)	fledge (3.1.28)
bankrout (3.1.41)	smug (3.1.43)	dimensions (3.1.56)	affections (3.1.57)
break (3.1.108)	bespeak (3.1.119)	merchandise (3.1.121)	beshrow (3.2.14)
naughty (3.2.18)	eche (3.2.23)	enforced (3.2.33)	flourish (3.2.49)
dismay (3.2.61)	fray (3.2.62)	fancy (3.2.63)	excrement (3.2.87)
redoubted (3.2.88)	crisped (3.2.92)	wanton (3.2.93)	dowry (3.2.95)
guiled (3.2.97)	meager (3.2.104)	scant (3.2.112)	surfeit (3.2.114)
counterfeit (3.2.115)	demigod (3.2.115)	faster (3.2.123)	prize (3.2.141)
account (3.2.155)	livings (3.2.156)	account (3.2.157)	presage (3.2.173)
intermission (3.2.199)	roof (3.2.204)	infidel (3.2.218)	shrowd (3.2.243)
state (3.2.259)	mere (3.2.262)	present (3.2.273)	confound (3.2.276)
magnificoes (3.2.280)	deface (3.2.299)	fond (3.3.9)	bootless (3.3.20)
forfeitures (3.3.22)	commodity (3.3.27)	griefs (3.3.32)	bated (3.3.32)
creditor (3.3.34)	conceit (3.4.2)	amity (3.4.3)	lover (3.4.7)
egal (3.4.13)	purchasing (3.4.20)	husbandry (3.4.25)	tranect (3.4.53)
habit (3.4.60)	accomplished (3.4.61)	prettier (3.4.64)	reed (3.4.67)
lewd (3.4.80)	enow (3.5.21)	rasher (3.5.24)	jealious (3.5.28)
honest (3.5.41)	grace (3.5.44)	lay (3.5.79)	

© Novel Units, Inc.

19

All rights reserved

Discussion Questions

1. What do you notice about the settings and scenes in this act? *(Scenes that focus on Portia alternate with scenes that spotlight Shylock.)* Why do you suppose Shakespeare alternates a scene featuring Portia with a scene about Shylock? What are some of the contrasts between Portia and Shylock? *(Portia is witty, warm, cordial, wealthy through inheritance; Shylock is bitter, angry, a wealthy money-lender.)*

2. What is Shylock's reaction to his daughter's flight? *(fury)* Would you say he is as concerned about the loss of his goods as the loss of his daughter? Do you have any sympathy for him? Why do you think Shakespeare includes the detail about Leah's ring? There is some disagreement among critics about who "Leah" is. What do you think? How does another ring figure in the story—at the end of the act? *(Portia gives her ring to Bassanio.)*

3. When does Shylock learn about Antonio's ships in relation to when he discovers his daughter's flight? *(He learns about Antonio's problem after he discovers Jessica's departure.)* Do you think he would have been so intent on getting his pound of flesh if Jessica hadn't left him?

4. Are you surprised that Portia so quickly offers to give money to someone she has never met? What does this show about her? Why do you suppose Bassanio didn't ask her for the money in the first place?

5. How does Launcelot feel about Jessica's conversion? *(He fears for her; thinks she is damned.)* What does he mean about Lorenzo helping drive up the price of pork? Explain the cause-effect sequence. *(Lorenzo was the cause of Jessica's becoming a Christian—"pork-eater;" the more pork-eaters there are, the higher the demand for pork, and the higher the cost.)*

6. What do you make of Lorenzo's comment about the Moorish woman (3.5.38)? *(Lorenzo accuses Launcelot of getting a Moorish woman pregnant.)* Why do you think Shakespeare included this detail—or is it perhaps an extemporaneous detail that has no dramatic purpose?

7. Myths about Jews abounded in Shakespeare's day. Does the idea of Shylock's wanting a pound of Christian flesh echo any of these? (Some students may be reminded of the myth that Jews ate Christian children.) Do you think he would really follow through on cutting Antonio?

8. How are you affected by the famous "Hath not a Jew eyes" speech? Does this speech make you feel for Shylock—or does it ring false? (Many people are moved by the speech and believe that through it, Shakespeare is saying that "Jews are people, too"; others find the plea less convincing, especially since a few lines later Shylock is plotting revenge.) Why do you suppose Shakespeare has chosen the synogogue for their meeting place? (It seems ironic that Shylock would arrange to discuss the details of this merciless plot with Tubal at the synogogue—the place of Jewish worship.)

9. If you could ask Jessica one question at this point, what would it be? What about Portia? Bassanio?

Prediction
Why is Portia disguising herself and Nerissa?

Supplementary Activities

Literary Analysis: Malapropism
A **malapropism** is the act or habit of misusing words ridiculously, especially by the confusion of words that are similar in sound. The word "malpropism" is derived from the character, Mrs. Malaprop, a woman in Sheridan's play, The Rivals, who makes a lot of word blunders. Dickens created a number of characters famous for their malapropisms.

Explain that Shakespeare often puts malapropisms in the mouths of certain characters—for laughs. For instance, Launcelot says, "Certainly the Jew is the very devil incarnation," when he means "incarnate" (2.2.27).

Have students point out other malapropisms (e.g.,2.2.124, "infection" /affection; line 133,"frutify"/signify; and line 136,"impertinent"/pertinent; 3.5.5, "agitation"/cogitation) and keep their eyes out for malapropisms in future scenes.

Ask students for recent-day examples of individuals known for their malapropisms (e.g., the animated character Homer Simpson; the character Archie Bunker from "All in the Family," a 60's/70's sit-com; and cartoon characters featured in the strip, "Shoe"). Have students list some of the malapropisms they have heard—in school, on the street, on TV, etc.

Proverb
A **proverb** is a short popular saying, usually of unknown origin, that expresses some common-place truth or useful thought. Point out the proverb to which Shakespeare has the Prince of Morocco refer in 2.7.65, "All that glisters is not gold." Have students talk about what that proverb means. (Sometimes the most appealing, evidently valuable things are not actually worth much.)

Pun
A **pun** is a play on words based on the similarity of sound between two words with different meanings. Point out Bassanio's pun on "lightest" (meaning "least heavy" as well as "least unchaste") 3.2.91. Have students list and explain other puns they find in the play. (e.g.,1.1.98—dam/damn; 1.2.87-88—best/beast; and 2.4.34 gentle/gentile).

Writing Ideas
1. Choose a proverb you think Shylock would like and explain why.

2. Describe Leah's ring from two different points of view—Shylock's and Jessica's. [For example: a) an interior monologue revealing Shylock's memories of Leah and the ring; and b) Jessica's comments to Lorenzo about the ring, after she trades it.]

Act IV

Scene I: At the court in Venice, the Duke tries to appeal to Shylock's sense of mercy, but Shylock demands his pound of flesh. Portia appears, dressed as a doctor of laws. She, too, tries to get Shylock to be merciful. When she is unsuccessful, she tries to get him to accept the money that Bassanio is offering. When he again refuses, she tells him to take the flesh—but points out that he is not entitled to any blood, and must take exactly one pound. If he draws any blood or misjudges the amount of flesh, he dies and his goods are confiscated. Shocked, Shylock says he will take the money. Portia drops another bombshell: Since he is an alien who has attempted to take the life of a citizen, Antonio is entitled to half his goods and the state, the other; his life is at the Duke's mercy. Although Gratiano is all for killing Shylock, the Duke spares his life. Antonio says that he is willing to show mercy: he wants half of Shylock's money to go to Lorenzo on Shylock's death and he wants Shylock to convert to Christianity. Shylock says that he is "content." Portia (disguised) refuses the Duke's invitation to dinner and refuses payment, but asks Bassanio for his gloves and ring as remembrances. Bassanio explains that the ring is from his wife, but decides to part with it.

Scene II: Gratiano brings Portia (still disguised) the ring and Nerissa (also disguised) gets her own ring from Gratiano.

Vocabulary

dram (4.1.6)	qualify (4.1.7)	remorse (4.1.20)	strange (4.1.20)
loose (4.1.24)	baned (4.1.46)	lodged (4.1.60)	fretten (4.1.77)
draw (4.1.87)	parts (4.1.92)	meetest (4.1.115)	envy (4.1.126)
inexecrable (4.1.128)	fell (4.1.135)	dam (4.1.136)	let (4.1.162)
difference (4.1.170)	throughly (4.1.172)	danger (4.1.179)	strained (4.1.183)
tenure (4.1.234)	balance (4.1.254)	process (4.1.273)	just (4.1.326)
substance (4.1.327)	estimation (4.1.330)	predicament (4.1.356)	rehearsed (4.1.361)
recant (4.1.390)			

Discussion Questions

1. What plan does Portia come up with for outsmarting Shylock in court? *(Portia disguises herself as a lawyer and uses the fact that he is an alien plotting the death of a citizen against him.)* Where else in Shakespeare have you seen women disguising themselves as men? What do you think would have happened if the intended lawyer had argued the case? Does the courtroom scene remind you of any recent real-life situations? In what sense did the outcome in Shylock's case hinge on a "technicality"? *(The contract became invalid only because blood would have been spilled—something not specifically mentioned in the contract.)* Do you think justice was served?

2. What role does the Duke play in this act? *(He is an arbiter, responsible for upholding the law—however little he may like the consequences.)* What appeal does he try to make to Shylock? *(He tries to appeal to Shylock's sense of mercy.)*

3. What do you make of Shylock's answer, when the Duke asks why he won't just settle for the money? Is his dislike of Antonio really similar to that of someone who simply doesn't like cats or pigs or bagpipes? Is it really true that he can't give any reason for his hatred? *(For some reason, he avoids admitting that he hates Antonio for the way Antonio has treated him—in business and as a Jew.)* Why do you suppose he doesn't talk about the way Antonio has spat on him and bad-mouthed his race?

4. What do you think of Portia's "quality of mercy" speech? How does it compare with what the Duke has said? *(She elaborates on the idea that even if you have justice on your side, you should show compassion.)* Why do you think it is so famous? Do you agree with it? What real people have demonstrated the quality of mercy she describes? Did Portia really expect Shylock to be moved by this speech? Why didn't she just "cut to the chase"—and point out that the law was actually on Antonio's side? Was she playing cat and mouse with him?

5. How does Shylock end up leaving court with less than he had when he went in? *(As punishment for planning an act that could have killed a citizen, Shylock loses his money—and is forced to convert to Christianity.)* Do you think this is fair? Would Portia's argument have worked if Shylock had not been Jewish? Do you think Shakespeare intends for us to feel that by forcing Shylock to convert, he is being "saved"—or are we meant to feel sympathy for him, since he is being required to give up his faith? Knowing what you do of Shylock, do you think he will secretly continue to practice his faith?

6. The Duke introduces Bellario as "a learned doctor whom I have sent for to determine this." (4.1.105-106) How do you suppose Portia knew that the Duke would send for Bellario? How do you suppose she convinced Bellario to send her the papers and the robes?

7. In one film version of the play (with Laurence Olivier), when Portia (disguised as the lawyer) asks, "Is your name Shylock?" (4.1.174) she is addressing Antonio, not Shylock. Why do you think this change was made? Does it suggest that Shylock is a man like any other Christian man in the room, who could be mistaken for them—in a way that Shakespeare's original does not? Do you think it enriches the play—or distorts it—when changes like this are made in various productions?

8. Why do both Bassanio and Gratiano say they would give up their wives? Were they prompted or asked to say so? *(No, they are simply expressing their devotion to Antonio and their desire to save him.)* What does this show about them? What is their wives' reaction to these declarations? *(Both are annoyed.)* Why do the men give up their rings? *(Their wives—in disguise—ask for the rings in payment for saving Antonio.)* Why do you think the wives trick them into doing so? Why does Shakespeare mix these details with the somber business at hand—essentially, the decision whether Antonio will be forced to give up his life? Is it just for comic effect? Is there some deeper significance?

9. If you could give one character in this act one piece of advice, what would it be?

Prediction
How will Gratiano and Bassanio explain the loss of their rings to their wives?

Supplementary Activities

Literary Analysis: Suspension of Disbelief
Suspension of disbelief refers to the reader's/viewer's willingness to accept the author's imaginative world without questioning how accurate it is. For an audience to suspend disbelief, plot and characters need to be believable and consistent. *The Merchant of Venice* has a fairy-tale like quality where the strange and wonderful happen. Ask for examples in this act (e.g., beautiful Portia disguised—and accepted—as a young judge; the miser's daughter, Jessica, finding happiness by marrying a Christian).
Ask: Why is the audience willing to accept these rather illogical turn-arounds?

Aside
An **aside** is a part of an actor's lines supposedly not heard by others on the stage. Point out the asides at the end of Act 4, Scene 2, and discuss their functions. Why do Portia and Nerissa speak in asides? (Portia and Nerissa don't want their husbands to know about the ring-trick they are plotting.)

Comic Relief
Sometimes a playwright includes an amusing incident or speech in a serious scene to "lighten up" the mood and provide some relief from the tension.
Ask: How does Shakespeare use comic relief to lighten the mood of the trial scene, in spots? (e.g., Bassanio and Gratiano both unknowingly irk their wives by saying they would give up their wives to save Antonio.)

Writing Ideas
1. Write an editorial about the Shylock/Antonio court case. Provide readers with brief background on the case and give your opinion about whether justice was served.

2. You are a reporter. Question both Shylock and Portia (in disguise) as they leave the court. Write up your interview in Q&A form.

Act V

Scene I: In a garden near Portia's house, Lorenzo and Jessica declare their love for each other. A messenger arrives with the news that Portia is on her way. Launcelot enters with news that Bassanio will be arriving soon. Musicians strike up and Portia and Nerissa show up. Portia tells Nerissa to go in and order the servants to say nothing when Bassanio arrives about Portia's absence. Soon thereafter Bassanio, Antonio, and Gratiano do arrive and Gratiano and Nerissa soon argue about the missing ring. Gratiano reveals that Bassanio has given up his ring, too, and Portia pretends to be angry. She gives the ring to Antonio to give to Bassanio, who is amazed to see that it is the one he lost. Portia reveals that she was the lawyer and Nerissa, the clerk—then gives Antonio the good news that three of his argosies are safe, after all. Nerissa gives Lorenzo some good news, too: he and Jessica will inherit Shylock's property after his death. Portia suggests that, although it is almost morning, they go inside and fill each other in on recent events. Gratiano, however, wants to ask Nerissa if she wouldn't rather spend the remaining couple of nighttime hours in bed with him.

Vocabulary

waft (5.1.11)	steal (5.1.15)	shrow (5.1.21)	patens (5.1.59)
quiring (5.1.62)	wanton (5.1.71)	rage (5.1.81)	spoils (5.1.85)
affections (5.1.87)	substitute (5.1.94)	tucket (5.1.121)	gelt (5.1.144)
posy (5.1.148)	respective (5.1.156)	scrubbed (5.1.162)	unkind (5.1.175)
mad (5.1.176)	fault (5.1.186)	civil doctor (5.1.210)	wealth (5.1.249)
advisedly (5.1.253)	amazed (5.1.266)	road (5.1.288)	

Discussion Questions

1. What role does music play in this final scene? *(Musicians start to play as Lorenzo and Jessica talk; they discuss their different responses to music.)*

2. How do Portia and Nerissa react when they "learn" that their rings are gone? *(angry)* Do their husbands try to make up good excuses for the losses? *(No, they tell the truth.)* Are you surprised? How do they learn the truth? *(Their wives produce the rings, and tease their husbands, implying that they have slept with the men who returned the rings—before admitting the trick they've played.)*

3. Would you say this is a happy ending for Antonio? Do you think he has gotten over the depression he seemed to be experiencing at the beginning? Is it a happy ending for Nerissa and Lorenzo? for Shylock? Do you think he will ever be reconciled with his daughter?

4. On what note does the play end? The Olivier film version contains an epilogue. A pensive Jessica stands alone while Kaddish (Jewish funeral) music is heard in the background. How does the final mood of the film contrast with Shakespeare's version?

Prediction

How do you suppose Portia and Bassanio will be doing five years from now? What about Nerissa and Gratiano? Jessica and Lorenzo? Will Shylock have changed?

Supplementary Activities

Literary Analysis: Comedy/Tragedy
In tragedy, there is often a sense that humans are inevitably doomed to suffer; the tragic hero faces defeat with dignity. Some critics see Shylock as a tragic hero, of sorts—someone who has been spat upon all of his life and is now undergoing a forced conversion.

The Merchant of Venice is considered a comedy, however. (Comedy presents the amusing spectacle of people's limitations.) In the context of the anti-Semitism of Elizabethan times, Antonio certainly regards Shylock's forced conversion as a way of saving Shylock from himself. Ask students who they feel the central character is—the one from whose point of view the events are seen. (Portia) Ask students how the mood of the play at the end returns to the comedic. (The teasing of the men about the rings restores the comic mood; Gratiano's final speech brings a laugh.)

Literary Analysis: Allusions

An **allusion** is a brief reference to a historical or literary figure, event, or object. To be effective, an allusion must tap the knowledge of the audience—who, in Shakespeare's day, could be expected to know something about mythical figures. Help students find and research allusions in Act 5, Scene 1:

- Troilus and Cressida, 4-6
- Thisbe, 10
- Dido, 10
- Medea, 13
- Erebus, 87

Writing Ideas

1. Shylock does not appear in the final act. Write a one-page scene in which you imagine where he goes and what he does after leaving the court.

2. Describe an alternative ending Shakespeare might have given the play.

Post-Reading Discussion/Writing Questions

1. Why do you think so many people feel that this play is anti-Semitic? Do you agree with them? What is your opinion of the idea that Shakespeare was actually taking a stand against anti-Semitism by pointing out how Venetian society mistreated Jews like Shylock? Do you see Shylock as a victim? cruel, vengeful person? greedy materialist? wronged father?

2. What do you make of the friendship between Antonio and Bassanio? Why is Antonio so willing to help Bassanio out financially? Why do you suppose Antonio's other friends aren't leaping to help him? Are Antonio and Bassanio each "good friends" to the other—or did Bassanio take advantage of Antonio? Why is Antonio feeling so low in the beginning? Has that changed by the end?

3. What are your impressions of Portia and Nerissa? In what ways do they mirror one another?

4. What do you think of Shylock's daughter, Jessica? Does Shylock love his daughter? How is her situation like Portia's? What decisions does she make? What does this show about her values? Was she justified in stealing from her father? Has she betrayed him by leaving—or does she deserve to "escape"? What does the fact that she and Lorenzo "blew" the money quickly on their honeymoon show you about them?

5. Which do you think are the key dramatic scenes in the play? What does the scene with the suitors/caskets show about Portia—and about her father's values? How did Shylock's "Hath not a Jew eyes" speech affect you? What about Portia's "mercy" speech? Which scenes made you laugh? Did any move you?

6. Why do you think Shakespeare entitled his play, The Merchant of Venice? Who is the merchant? Is Shylock the central character?

7. Why does Antonio dislike Shylock so much? Why does Shylock hate Antonio so much? Do you think anything could ever change the way they feel about each other?

8. What did you learn about Shakespearean language from this play? Which lines did you find most "pleasing to the ear"?

9. Some people object to teaching this play on the grounds that it is anti-Semitic, saying that it is by the quintessential "DWEM" (dead white European male) and that there are many contemporary multicultural works that are more appropriate for today's students. Others disagree. What do you think?

10. Which role in *The Merchant of Venice* would you most like to play? Why?

11. Does this remind you of any of Shakespeare's other plays? For example, in which other plays do you find women disguising themselves as men?

12. In this play, who are the victims? Who are the "bad guys"? Are there any "repentant ones"?

13. Do you think Shylock was treated decently, in the end?

14. How do the three inscriptions on the chests apply to the action throughout the play? Who got what he/she desired? deserved? Who gave and hazarded all they had?

15. In discussions with other students, did you discover any different points of view on the play? How do you account for that?

16. Does this play call to mind any other poem, play, film, story? Does it remind you of any personal experiences? anything you have read in a recent newspaper or heard about on the TV news? What parallels do you see, for example, between Jessica (who marries a Christian) and her present-day counterparts (Jews who marry non-Jews)?

17. During discussions of the play, how did your understanding/feelings about it change? How would you describe the way discussion helped you think about the play? Did you find yourself examining your own memories? Did you find yourself reacting to others' observations?

Post-Reading Extension Activities

Note to Teachers
For a variety of professional services, teachers should be aware of the Folger Shakespeare Library, 201 East Capital Street, S.E., Washington DC 20003 (202-544-7077). An annotated bibliography of approximately 190 readily available books about Shakespeare and his age for children in grades 4-8 can be ordered for $5.00. The staff provides tours, assists schools in planning Shakespeare festivals, and conducts a high-school fellowship program. For information, write or call Peggy O'Brien.

Resources for Teachers
1. Criticism
Shakespeare and the Jews. James Shapiro, Columbia University Press, 1996.
Merchant of Venice. Jay C. Halio, Oxford University Press. (Includes a stage history of the play in Israel.)
The Merchant. Wesker. (About Shylock—a counterpoint to the anti-Semitism of Shakespeare's play.)
The Jew of Malta. Christopher Marlowe. (A distinctly anti-Semitic play by Shakespeare's contemporary. Compare Barabas and Shylock.)
Shylock and the Jewish Question. Martin Yaffe, Johns Hopkins University Press, 1997. (Presents a counterargument to the more common one that, in *The Merchant of Venice*, Shakespeare reflects the anti-Semitism typical of his day.)
Shakespeare Set Free (Volume 1) ed. by Peggy O'Brien.

2. Websites
http://ericir.syr.edu/
AskERIC InfoGuide: Teaching Shakespeare
Search the Virtual Library—AskERIC Infoguides
Search for TEACHING SHAKESPEARE
This is an excellent site—Internet sources, Listservs; anything you want on teaching Shakespeare you will find here.

http://www.rdg.ac.uk/globe/
This is a wonderful website that provides information on the Globe Theatre and its reconstruction—now reopened to the public after 400 years! It includes illustrations and texts on staging at the original Globe as well as a news bulletin and links to other Shakespeare sites.

http://www.shakespearemag.com
A gem for teachers looking for ideas on how to teach Shakespeare; contains an excellent essay on dealing with the anti-Semitism of *The Merchant of Venice* in the classroom.

http://starbuck.com/shakespeare/TheMerchanthall/wwwboard.html
A light discussion group—for lurking or participating

http://the-tech.mit/edu/Shakespeare/Comedy/
For an online version of the play, complete with hypertext

http://www.geocities.com/Athens/Acropolis/7221/
Shakespeare and anti-Semitism

3. Viewing
Literary Masterpieces (ITC, 1970): "The Merchant of Venice" (set in the 1860's) with Laurence Olivier as Shylock, Joan Plowright as Portia (Olivier's real-life wife), and Jeremy Irons (formerly Sherlock Holmes on PBS) as Bassanio.

Check for local performances of *The Merchant of Venice* so that students can attend a live performance!

"Teaching Shakespeare: New Approaches from the Folger Shakespeare Library" (Zenger Media 800/421-4246)

4. Further Student Reading/Viewing for Comparison
Shakespeare's comedies: *As You Like It, All's Well That End's Well, Comedy of Errors, The Taming of the Shrew*

Writing

1. Essay topics

- the theme of loss (of wives, lives, money, etc.) as it is developed throughout the play
- Agree or disagree: "Portia is the least lovable of Shakespeare's comedy heroines."
- Jessica as villain
- Jessica as foil for Shylock
- comparison/contrast of Portia and Jessica
- comparison/contrast of Portia and Kate (*The Taming of the Shrew*)
- Gratiano as the play's jester
- comparison/contrast (after viewing) of two actors' portrayals of Shylock (such as Laurence Olivier's and Warren Mitchell's)
- Analyze the dramatic function of the debate between Antonio and Shylock over whether Jacob had the right to Laban's sheep. How did their argument reflect a central theme in the play?
- Compare and contrast the Prince of Aragon and Shylock. How did they both consider themselves "deserving"?
- Why do you think Shakespeare had Jessica exchange the ring for a monkey? Is she just another newlywed on a shopping spree?
- Compare the Launcelot/Gobbo scene with the casket trial.
- Research source materials used by Shakespeare, starting with Marlow's *The Jew of Malta*. (You might find Kenneth Muir's *The Sources of Shakespeare's Plays* helpful.)
- hypocrisy, greed, and hatred as motivating forces in the play
- the values upheld by the main characters: Portia, Antonio, Bassanio, Shylock, Jessica
- Shylock: only what the Christians around him made him be
- analysis of the "Hath not a Jew eyes" speech; Could this speech be meant to diminish Shylock?
- Develop the following thesis statement: "Throughout the play, Portia and Shylock stand in counterpoint to each other."
- Support or refute one of the following statements:
  "*The Merchant of Venice* is more of a tragedy than a comedy."
  "*The Merchant of Venice* is not just anti-Semitic, it is anti-religion in general."
- the fairytale-like nature of *The Merchant of Venice*
- juxtaposition of contrasting scenes throughout the play (e.g., alternation of Portia's and Shylock's scenes)
- reversal of fortune in the courtroom scene
- the final scene—a happy ending...or a bitterly ironic one?
- Support the idea that in *The Merchant of Venice*—as in most of Shakespeare's plays— nearly every line somehow supports the play's theme.

2. Newspaper

Recreate the front page of a newspaper that alludes to significant developments in the play (e.g., Portia's engagement, the loss of Antonio's ships, Shylock's court case). Don't forget to name the paper, give the weather report, and provide a summary of what's inside (e.g., theater and the arts, Dear Abby). Try to come up with some snappy, sensationalistic headlines.

3. Headlines

Create newspaper headlines for each scene in the play.

4. Letter

Write a letter to one of the characters telling him or her about a similar situation you were in or giving them advice. For example, what might you say to Antonio about borrowing money from people?

5. Newspaper Article

Write a newspaper piece based on one of the events or situations in the play—such as Portia/Bassanio's engagement, a cartoon based on the scene where the suitors choose among the coffers, an editorial about anti-Semitism, an advertisement for Shylock's services.

6. Poem

Respond to one of the scenes with a poem one of the characters might write. For example, what love poem—perhaps in the form of a Shakespearean sonnet—might Bassanio, Gratiano, or Lorenzo write for his loved one? What bitterness poem might Shylock write? What confession poems might Portia and Nerissa write?

7. Film Review

View a video of the play (such as the version with Laurence Olivier) and critique it. Alternatively, compare and contrast two film versions of the same scene. Which is closer to Shakespeare's intent?

8. Journal Entries

Assume the persona of one of the main characters—such as Portia or Shylock. Write several journal entries in which you react to events that occur in the play.

9. Dream Diary

Assume the persona of one of the characters in the play. Describe a dream that character might have at some point in the story, e.g., what might Antonio dream when he finds out that his ships are lost and he must forfeit on his loan?

10. "How to" Article

You are Portia. Write an article for a leading women's magazine on "how to choose a husband."

11. Describing a Place

Describe Portia's or Shylock's favorite place.

12. Contemporary Setting

Choose a scene from *The Merchant of Venice* and rewrite it in:
a) modern English
b) a present-day setting.

13. Actor's Diary

After researching Elizabethan times, pretend to be an actor in Shakespeare's day who played ____(a character in *The Merchant of Venice*). In your diary, reflect on your life—both in the theatre (the people in your audience, what you like/don't like about your role, how you are preparing for it, costume you wear, etc.) and outside of it (e.g., recreational activities, food).

14. Letter

After learning what the Globe was like, pretend that you had been there to see a performance of *The Merchant of Venice* about 400 years ago. Write a letter to your friend about what the experience was like.

15. Soap Opera Script

Recast a scene from *The Merchant of Venice* as a soap opera script (for an actual or fictional soap opera).

16. Tragedy

The Merchant of Venice could have been quite tragic, with a few plot twists. Outline your version of *The Merchant of Venice*—the tragedy.

17. Alternative Setting

Shakespearean plays are often adapted and placed in alternative settings. In the film version of *The Merchant of Venice* starring Laurence Olivier, for instance, the story takes place in 19th-century Venice. Imagine another time and place in which you might set the story if you were the director. Briefly describe the sets and costumes you would need.

18. ListServ Posting

Pretend that you have joined a Shakespeare discussion group on the Internet. Respond to the following posting by another member, John Smith.

"It is misguided to label Shakespeare 'anti-Semitic.' Despite Shakespeare's characterization of Shylock, he does not portray all Jews as villains (e.g., Jessica)..."

(As you will see if you look at some examples of actual ListServ postings, most responses begin by quoting, in italics, the original posting.) Your response might supply details that support or contradict the idea that Jessica is villainous. You might also consider how Launcelot and his father are portrayed.

Listening/Speaking

1. Act Out

Act out selected scenes in the play (ultimately, if possible, for other classes or even parents). To prepare for this, students might do one or more of the following:

a) Create a chart showing which characters are onstage during various scenes.

b) Use fabric scraps to design costumes for various characters.

c) Create casting cards for various roles (What is the casting team looking for in a Portia? a Shylock? an Antonio?) and stage a casting interview.

d) Share with students one of the parodies of Shakespearean language done by Mark Twain or James Thurber; discuss with students what these writers are poking fun at (Shakespeare's overelaborate speech, his unusual use of apparently familiar words, etc.).

2. Interview

Several characters in the play express their ideas about commitment. Stage a discussion like the one a host like Oprah Winfrey might set up. ("When is it okay to break a promise?") "Guests" might include Shylock, Jessica, Bassanio, Antonio, Gratiano. The interviewer introduces the topic and questions the entire group. Audience members direct particular questions at individual guests. (Audience members should prepare their questions as homework.)

3. Debate

Choose one of these statements and hold a classroom debate.

- Portia is prejudiced.
- Portia/Bassanio and Jessica/Lorenzo will still be happily married ten years later.
- The court's decision is unfair to Shylock.

Have students debate the relative merits of the essays reprinted after the text of *The Merchant of Venice* (by Nicholas Rowe, William Hazlitt, Anonymous, Elmer Stoll, Linda Bamber, Alexander Leggatt, and Sylvan Barnet). (Essays might be divided among student groups.)

4. Perform

Sponsor memorization contests and activities. Who can memorize the longest passage in the play? Spend five minutes each day having the entire class memorize a choral reading.

5. Compete

Organize a "Jeopardy"-like game with "Famous Quotations from *The Merchant of Venice*."

6. Evaluate

Have students choose a favorite speech from the play and memorize it (five lines or more). Then get into small groups and recite lines. Have other members of the group comment on performances with regard to accuracy, expression, and tone.

7. Discuss

Choose your favorite scene. Discuss it in a small group. What problem is raised? What do each of the characters want? What do you learn about each character from what he/she says? Improvise the scene (e.g., put it into everyday English).

8. Drama

a. Improvise a scene from the play as if it were an episode from a sitcom or soap opera. Suppose, for example, that you decide to do a scene where Portia and Nerissa discuss Bassanio and Gratiano. If this were an episode of "Saved by the Bell" or "Clueless" or "Sabrina" or "The Young and the Restless," who might the Shakespearean-equivalent characters be? Where would they be having this conversation? What would happen?

b. With several classmates, stage a "tableau"—a scene from *The Merchant of Venice* where the players freeze in place. (The court-room scene would be a good one to try.) The relationship between the players should be indicated through gestures and facial expressions. Players pick out a simple costume or prop—such as a hat—that conveys the character's personality and/or social position. Classmates can guess the scene and characters. This activity can be used as the basis for a bulletin board display: Students stage several tableaux representing different points of the story, have a classmate photograph each, and add captions.

c. Improvise one of the following scenes using sounds only (no words); then pantomime the same scene.
   a) Shylock agrees to lend Bassanio the money.
   b) Portia's suitors undergo the coffer test.
   c) Jessica disguises herself and runs away with Lorenzo.
   d) Portia confronts Shylock in court.
   e) Bassanio and Gratiano lose their rings.

d. Come up with a version of *The Merchant of Venice* that might appear on one of your favorite weekly TV shows. For example, what about a "Hercules" episode with Hercules/Lolus transformed into Antonio/Bassanio—or a "Xena the Warrior" show with Xena and Gabrielle as Portia and Nerissa?

e. According to experts, the best way to nurture a love for Shakespeare is to take students to live productions. Do your best to arrange for students to see a live performance of *The Merchant of Venice*—or at least one of the comedies.

f. Consider participation in a student Shakespeare Festival. For example, at the Folger Theater in Washington, DC, over a six-day period every year students from 50 schools have half an hour to perform Shakespeare on the Elizabethan-era stage for one another, parents, and the festival judges. (Call 202-675-0395 for information.) For assistance in planning your own festival, call the Folger (202-544-7077).

g. Choose a particular character and summarize selected scenes from that character's point of view. (Be sure to explain how you know what you know.)

h. Write a scene that occurs offstage (such as the scene where Nerissa and Lorenzo elope or where Portia and Nerissa travel to the court, in disguise). Alternatively, write a scene that didn't happen in the play—but might have. (For instance, what might have happened if, in the middle of the courtroom scene, Bassanio had recognized Portia?)

i. Divide the class into five groups, each group responsible for one act. Each group rewrites a scene from the act in modern English or in slang, then acts it out.

j. Rewrite a scene from *The Merchant of Venice* in a new setting (e.g., a shopping mall, "People's Court," Beverly Hills). Present it to the class.

Language Study

1. Comb the play for examples of the following:
   - allusions
   - malapropisms
   - puns
   - metaphors and similes
   - bawdy language
   - Shakespearean insults
   - words that mean something different now than in Shakespeare's day

2. Make a list of quotations from the play that have come into popular use.

3. Look in newspapers and magazines (headlines, ads, captions) for references to lines or situations from *The Merchant of Venice*.

4. Select three key words that you notice recur throughout *The Merchant of Venice* (e.g., "virtue," "lose," "cruelty"). Note where in the play each of the words occurs. (Using a Shakespeare CD or getting on the World Wide Web might make this easier.) Then prepare a "concordance" entry for each word. (Look at a concordance in your library's reference section for a model.) Explain what the word means in each context. Analyze how the repetition of each word contributes to the development of a particular theme.

Art

1. After looking at some scenes from the play illustrated by various artists (see Research activity, page 39), try illustrating a scene or two from the play, yourself. Use any medium you choose, such as markers, watercolor, collage, or plasticine. Caption your picture.

2. Capture your impressions of a famous quote from the play in a collage/montage. Cover a piece of posterboard with magazine cut-outs, drawings you have made, and/or small objects that connect with the quote. Put the quote at the top of the board in letters cut from a magazine (or stencilled).

3. Create paper bag or sock puppets for a scene from the play and act it out for younger students. (Alternatively, use paper-plate masks and wear them or mount them on a stick to hold in front of you while you act out the scene. Create a group mural—of Belmont, Shylock's house, the court, etc.—for your backdrop.)

4. Create a visual plot outline for the play. On the map you might illustrate what happened at key landmarks such as Belmont, Shylock's house, the court, etc.

5. Create a comic strip that shows a scene from *The Merchant of Venice*. If you like, use well-known comic strip characters who somehow resemble Shakespeare's.

6. Create a shoebox diorama that depicts a scene from the play.

7. Create a mobile of labeled objects that have significance in the play (e.g., rings, ducats, monkeys, a contract).

8. Think about how the three couples will feel about each other on their first Valentine's Day together. What will they appreciate about each other? What sort of cards might they make for each other? romantic ones? ones with a joking sentiment? ones with a sarcastic barb? To what specific situations in their courtship and marriage might each refer in the message?

Design the Valentine cards that one of the three couples might exchange on their first Valentine's Day together. To make a pop-up card:

a) Fold (stiff) paper in half.
b) Snip two parallel cuts in the fold. Snips should be an inch or so deep, an inch or two apart.
c) Open the card, put your finger through the slits and pull up to make a little "standing table."
d) Glue your cut-out to the front of the "table" so that it will pop up when the card is opened.
e) Illustrate the outside of the card and add a message or poem.

Music

1. Choose some contemporary songs the suitors or lovers in the play might sing. Prepare an oral presentation of the songs, discussing how they are related to the play.

2. Recast one of the scenes in the play as a "music video."

3. Tape a selection of pieces that you would use at various points in the play.

4. Listen to Randy Newman's "Dixie Flyer" about Jews in New Orleans during WWII. Do the lyrics remind you of Jessica and her father in any way?

Research

1. Several artists have illustrated scenes from *The Merchant of Venice*. Learn more about a book publisher named John Boydell who opened his Shakespeare Gallery in 1789—and changed the course of English painting by creating a market for "history painting." Find some of these paintings/drawings and learn more about the artists.

2. Create a timeline that sets the events in *The Merchant of Venice* against an historical backdrop. Include the status of Jews in England on your timeline.

3. Research some of the mythical and biblical allusions in the play.

4. Devise a questionnaire about women's rights and/or love and marriage. Include at least ten questions and try to get at some of the ideas expressed in the play (e.g., "Should decisions about what the wedding will be like be made equally by both partners?" "Do you think housework should be shared equally by husband and wife?") Administer the questionnaire, tally the answers, and write a short report on your findings. Report to the whole group on what you found—and what this shows about attitudes in our times—and in Shakespeare's.

5. Find out how German Nazis subverted *The Merchant of Venice* to their own ends.

6. Historically, how has Shylock been portrayed in various productions since Shakespeare's time? How are these productions a reflection of their times?

Current Events

1. Use resources such as the *Reader's Guide to Periodical Literature* or do a search on the Internet for news articles, advice columns, ads, comics, etc. that are somehow related to situations in *The Merchant of Venice* (e.g., displays of anti-Semitism, loan sharking, legal turn-arounds on technicalities, interfaith marriages). Create a bulletin board or poster of such items, with captions that explain the parallels with *The Merchant of Venice*.

2. Find references in newspapers and magazines to *The Merchant of Venice*. These might be reviews of stage productions, allusions in headlines, advertisements, etc. Create a poster display or scrapbook.

Assessment for *The Merchant of Venice*

Assessment is an on-going process, more than a quiz at the end of the book. Points for each project successfully completed may be placed in the "Teacher" column on the list below to show the level of achievement. Students should check off items as they complete them.

Name _____   Date_____

Student Teacher

_____ _____   1. As you read, keep a Response Log.

_____ _____   2. Write an epilogue or short-story sequel to *The Merchant of Venice*.

_____ _____   3. Participate in writing and performing a Reader's Theatre script for one scene from the play.

_____ _____   4. Write an essay about *The Merchant of Venice* using one of the topics on page 31.

_____ _____   5. Make a glossary of odd-sounding words from Shakespeare's day that you encounter in the play.

_____ _____   6. Choose a piece of music you would use as background music for the final scene of a radio-play version of *Merchant*, and write a one-paragraph explanation.

_____ _____   7. Do a dance improvisation or mime interpretation of one scene from the story.

_____ _____   8. Research the status of Jews in England during the 300 years prior to the play—and for 50 years afterward.

_____ _____   9. Write a poem in response to the story.

_____ _____   10. Alternate activity of your choice.

_____ _____   11. Write a self-evaluation of your portfolio, explaining its strengths and weaknesses, and assigning yourself an overall grade.

Note: For quizzes, tests, a study guide, and activity sheets focusing on critical thinking skills, vocabulary study, literary analysis, and writing skills, see the **Novel Units Student Packet** for *The Merchant of Venice*.